I LOVE DAD WHEN...

BY JERRY LLOYD-WILLIAMS AND 'STICKY CONTENT'
ILLUSTRATED BY PETER STANDLEY

Nightingale Press

an imprint of Wimbledon Publishing Company Ltd.
LONDON

ISBN: 1903222 53 2

Produced in Great Britain
Printed and bound in Hungary

…when he gets romantic. A couple of glasses of red over Sunday lunch, and suddenly he's regaling us with stories about when him and Mum used to go courting. "And when I finally got her onto my brand new Norton, she leant the wrong way going into all the corners…"

…when he forgets on purpose. He
constantly gets one of Mum's friends'
names wrong - the one he's never got on
with. "Top-up, Randy? I mean, Mandy…"
(Apparently, it all kicked off when she
queried his barbecue technique. Some
time in the summer of '72…)

...when he sits complaining in front of
Top of the Pops. "Call this music? I
could make a better noise in my garage!
Is that a boy or a girl? Honestly, you
just can't tell these days…"

…when he provides supplementary benefits. As soon as Mum isn't looking, he slips some extra cash into my hand. But when I try to thank him, he pretends not to know what I'm talking about.

...when he never forgets to crack
his favourite Christmas gag. Just as
the plates are being cleared away, he'll
shout to the person sitting furthest
away from him: "God, I'm full. Undo
me belt, will you? You're nearer."

…when he goes all cloak-and-dagger. For weeks before Mum's birthday, he sneaks around with a mad glint in his eye, chuffed to bits with all the pressies he's bought her on the sly. But then gets really disappointed when he finds out they're all the wrong size (again!).

Happy Birthday

…when he's one of the lads. Like when he rings and asks if I "fancy a couple of pints with the old man?"

…when he rises to the
occasion. Mum convinces him
that he's got the kind of 'Big Match
Temperament' needed to take care of all
the cooking for next week's dinner party. So
he goes into training for six days: researching
recipes, drawing up schedules, buying new
utensils, writing out orders for his
'assistants' and driving miles to pick
up obscure ingredients.

…when he gets all gooey. Give him a wedding, a few glasses of bubbly and an old *Righteous Brothers* number and within minutes he's smooching like a teenager with Mum.

…when he does his stand-up routine. He puts in some fake teeth, ruffles his hair and does an 'hilarious' Ken Dodd. Except it sounds more like Frank Carson and no one's ever quite sure whether they're laughing with him or at him.

...when he tries to stay with it. Half an hour later, at the same wedding, he attempts to jitterbug to *La Vida Loca* - and puts his back out for a week.

…when he's not vain about
his appearance. Just don't mention
if you've think he's had a haircut.
(Oh and by the way, it's not 'receding',
it's 'always been like that' - despite all
the old family photos which clearly
show otherwise.)

…when he sees life in terms
of sport. Like when I come home from
school with a bad maths mark and he
says: "You're going to have to show a
bit more commitment in the 50:50
challenges, son…"

…when he says he'll take us out -
'anywhere you like'! Only we always
end up in the same quiet country pub
that still brews its own beer, with just
a wooden-panelled fruit machine
for amusement.

...when he asks if I want to go
down to the shops with him to 'pick up
a couple of things for Mum'. It's a ten-
minute visit tops, but we end up having
lunch and talking about my old
boyfriends for hours...

...when he goes AWOL.
He says he's taking the dog for a
walk on Sunday afternoon, and
promptly disappears for three hours.
When he gets back, Spot is oddly frisky,
while Dad seems strangely drowsy and
is mumbling something about
'that bloody ref'.

...when he hands me the wheel.
After my sixteenth birthday, he took me
to a deserted car park every Sunday
and put up with me kangaroo-ing the
family estate around.

...he sends me a card out of the blue:
'I'm very proud of you. Love, Dad'.

…when he knows his way around.
He asks me which route I'm going to
take to get home and when I tell him
he says, "Ooh, I wouldn't go that way. I'd
have taken the A316 to Richmond,
turned right at Chiswick, then cut up
through Gunnersbury…"

…when he spins the 'platters that matter'. We're in the car going to visit relatives and he puts on what he thinks is a trendy CD - which means we have to sit listening to *Foreigner* or *REO Speedwagon* all the way there and all the way back…

Rock
Classics

…when he splashes it about. He
insists on paying for dinner, then talks
constantly about how expensive
everything was, how bad the service was,
how small the portions were…

…when he gets a bit fruity.
After an extravagant anniversary
dinner, he starts winking at Mum and
announces: "Last train to Scarborough
pier leaves leaves in fifteen minutes".
Then he staggers off to bed
giggling to himself…

…he tries to do his bit
around the house. After hours of
searching (and years of nagging) he
finally discovers where the Hoover is.
Two minutes into the job, he says "I'm not
getting enough suck out of this motor" and
decides to 'take a look under the bonnet'.
Four hours later, the dining room table is a
sea of fluffy debris, oily cogs and spare
washers - and Dad's promising to
buy a new cleaner in the
morning.

…when he says he doesn't
want a fuss. For weeks before his
birthday, he's telling everyone he
meets, "Don't do anything special - I'm
too old for birthdays nowadays".
But then, come the day, he gets all
moody when we pretend we haven't
organised anything…

…when he uses his legendary sense
of timing. Like when he decides to
wash out all his paint brushes in the
kitchen sink - an hour before Mum has
got fourteen people coming round for
drinks and a four-course dinner…

...when he gets all emotional.
When my GCSE results came
through, Mum jumped up and down for
joy, while Dad just said "That's my girl"
and rushed off, muttering about
'something in his eye'...

...when he proves he's
no technophobe. The Instant
Messenger on my laptop keeps
crashing my machine. As I howl abuse at
it, he leans over, turns off one of the
TCP/IP protocol converters (whatever that
is) and reboots the machine without a
problem. All this from the guy who
couldn't load up a ZX Spectrum
ten years ago.

...when he practises
what he preaches. He lectures
us all to be extra careful in
dangerous situations: driving on the
motorway, drilling through walls, flying
kites near overhead pylons etc. And
then he goes and almost chews through
the cable of his electric hedge
trimmers ... with his electric
hedge trimmers!

…when he takes it too
easy. He dithers around saying
we've got plenty of time to catch my
train - then suddenly notices the time,
sprints to the car in his slippers and sets off
down the drive like Nigel Mansell, with me
struggling to close the door before it hits the
gate. Okay, I nearly lose my arm every
time I come to stay, but I know he
wouldn't want to miss out on that
hi-octane ride to Paddock
Wood station.

STATION

…when he knows his limits.
Like when he sings dirty rugby songs
in the bath, but sings the rude words
really quietly when he hears Mum
coming upstairs…

…when he looks after
the pennies. He gets the 1970s
Christmas tree lights down from the
loft, spends three hours checking all the
bulbs, puts them on the tree, offers my
Mum the switch with a flourish … and they
don't work. Before she can say anything,
he mumbles: "No they're fine, must be a
loose connection somewhere" and
spends another three hours
checking the bulbs again.

...when he blows me
away with his past. Watching a
music programme on the telly, I
comment that I really like an obscure
blues guitarist, who is making a rare
appearance on the box. He disappears
upstairs, then returns with an album by
the same man and a ticket receipt
from his debut at the Chicago
Blues Festival, 1964.

…when we discover his soft
centre. Dad tells me to go into his
wallet to get some cash to pay the pizza
boy. As I pull out the dosh, a photo falls
out of his wallet. It's a picture of Mum, at
the seaside in a pretty summer dress. On
the back in his writing are the words,
'The day she said "yes"'.

…when he forgets about the
pounds. He's always saying, "Your
mother thinks I'm made of money, she
spends it like it's going out of fashion…"
- then arrives home the next day with yet
another hi-fi add-on, this one to reduce
mid-range static when recording
from tuner to mini-disc.

Hi-Fi

...when he fits in. I was dreading
him coming down the pub watching
football with all my mates. But within
half an hour we've all forgotten he's my
Dad, and he's shouting at the big screen
with the rest of us.

F.C.

…when he has a
spring clean. Dad asks me to
help him clear some of my old junk
out of the loft. We spend all day up
there, laughing constantly as we trawl
through box after box of stuff we used to
play with together. "We'll make more
space another day, if we have to,"
he says with dust in his hair and
a smile on his face.

FRAGILE

...when he beats all the other dads! The man who looks out of breath just watching a game of cricket wins a medal at my sports day. In front of everyone, all my mates and their parents, he's the runaway egg and spoon champ!

...when he covers for
me. Staggering home after my
first school disco - an hour late - he
pulls up and says "hop in". I puke on the
way home, but he stays really calm. Carrying
me upstairs, he puts me to bed with a big
glass of water and a bucket. Next morning,
the only thing my Mum wants to know
is why my best outfit is washed and
in the machine.

…when he takes us for a game of football in the park. He always has the youngest ones on his side, but still manages to win 20-12. Only the dog has better ball control…

…when he doesn't say "I told you so". When he finds me crying my eyes out in my bedroom, after I've been dumped again, he just gives me a cuddle. Even though he'd said all along that I should be careful with 'that one'.

…when he shows his macho
side. He's normally a calm man
who wouldn't say boo to a goose.
But when that bloke tried to break into
our garage, he chased him all the way
up the road, clobbered him with a
dustbin lid and sat on him till the
police came.

...when I realise his strength.
He's twice as old as I am, with
skinny arms that haven't seen any kind
of sport in decades, but when I
confidently challenge him to an arm-
wrestle it's only minutes before he has
me pinned to the table in defeat.

…when he tries to be one of
the lads. He came along to my stag
do, throwing money around and
threatening to 'drink everyone under the
table'. A couple of hours later, he's
wandering round the bar on his hands
and knees, giggling like a maniac
and trying to light his own farts.

STAG PARTY

...when he tries to help with
my homework. "Let me do it!"
he snaps, as I sit there scratching my
head over my advanced trigonometry
paper. Three hours later, he is still on the
phone to his science boffin mate,
trying to remember exactly what
cosine stands for.

...when he shows us what
matters. Like when we were at
grandad's funeral, he shouted out a joke,
which made everyone in the church laugh.
Someone turned to complain and he pulled
a funny face, saying: "He was my Dad! I
think I know how he'd want me to
behave." From five to fifty five, that's
one thing kids never forget.